Vicks from the Rotterdam Zoo

This is the story of Vicks, the polar bear cub who was born on December 6, 2010, in the Rotterdam Zoo, the Netherlands. His birth was a highly anticipated and special event, accompanied by lots of joy and excitement around the world. This book pays tribute to Vicks's first year of life, which we want to celebrate with everyone who has seen Vicks in person, through his webcam, and who may not have met him before. Most of all, this book is for anyone who wants to experience a polar bear cub's very first adventures.

With thanks to everyone who has made this book possible:
Zookeeper, Stefan Timmermans, who has recorded and shared all of
Vicks' adventures; photographer, Rob Doolaard, for his beautiful pictures;
JW Borleffs, Sander van der Wel, Cynthia den Uijl, Ronald van Oorschot and
Fedor Nap, who provided amazing photos in the Vicks photo competition;
and the employees of Blijdorp Communication, who have helped me in every way
possible to make this informative and entertaining book.

Mack

Vicks
The Polar Bear Cub

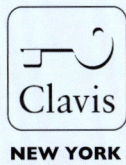

Clavis

NEW YORK

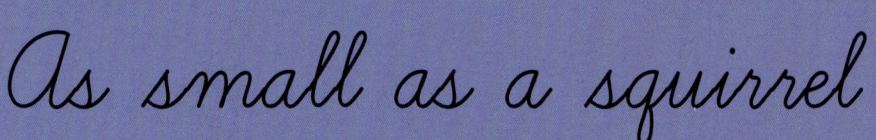

As small as a squirrel

Mother and cub in a dark and cozy den

Come and have a look. Do you see two polar bears sleeping? You only see one?

Take a good look and you'll see a little white ball. That's Vicks, the polar bear cub.

He's just been born and is helpless and small. He's as small as a squirrel.

Vicks is lying close to his mother, Olinka, who takes very good care of him.

For several months she will keep her baby inside this dark and cozy den

as he begins to grow.

Vicks can't see or hear anything

Polar bear cubs are born blind and deaf. The only thing little Vicks can do is drink his mother's rich, warm milk. Lots and lots of milk!

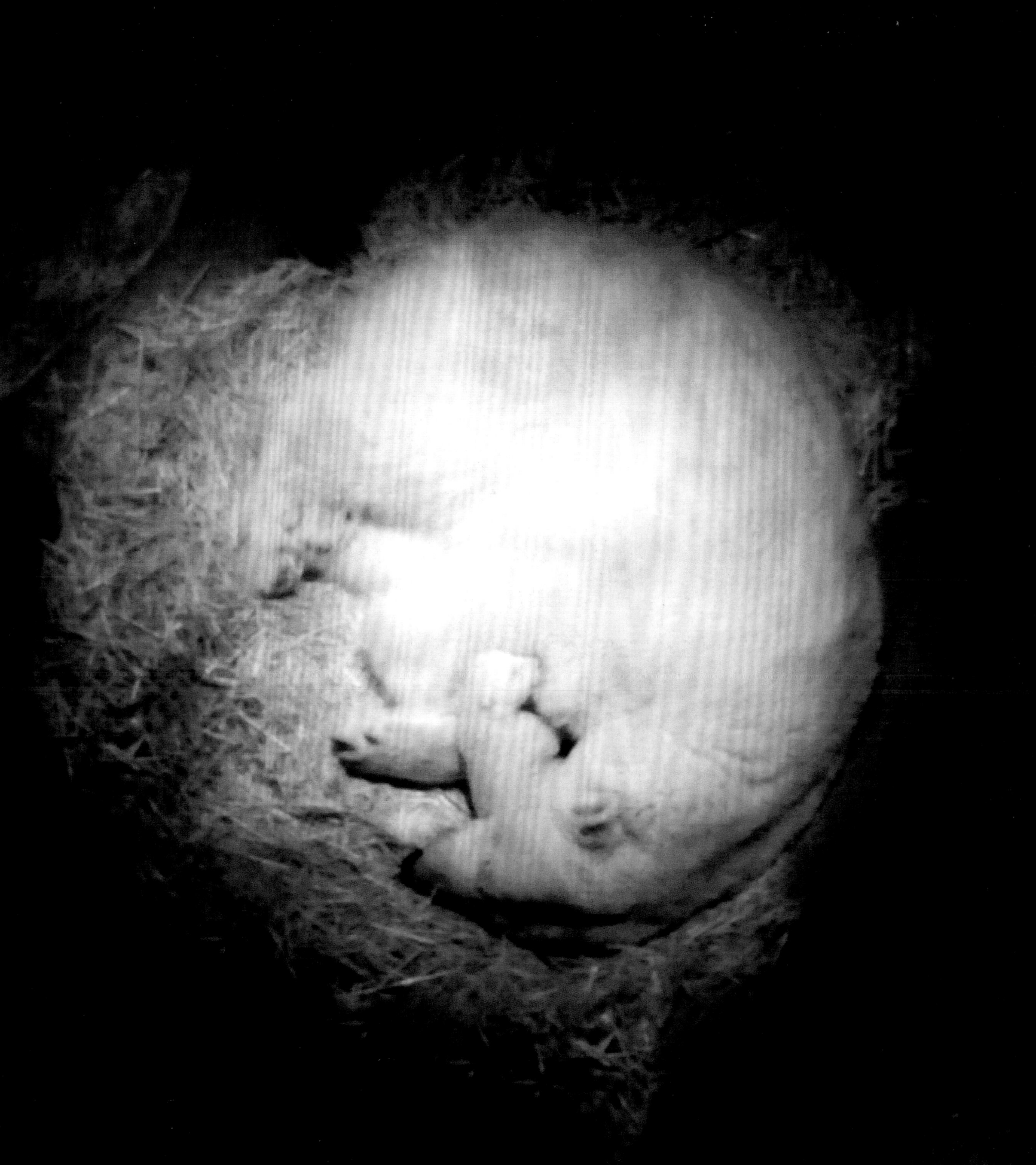

So much light!

Taking his first steps outside

Thanks to Olinka's nutritious milk, Vicks grows into a sturdy little cub who can see and hear very well. After several months, he is big and strong enough to leave his cozy den to go outside. Will it be dark there, too? No, so much light! Vicks is startled and closes his eyes. But he's curious, too.

The world is such a big place! There's so much to see and do.

It's like a giant playground. Cautiously, Vicks starts exploring. Hello, world!

Better than a penguin!

Vicks is strong enough to stand on his own legs. Step, step, step. He can immediately walk better than a penguin!

Everything is a little scary

In the beginning, everything is brand new for Vicks. For the very first time he sees ice and rocks, grass and water, clouds, and sky. It's all wonderful, but a little scary, too. Suddenly a crow flies in front of his nose. Vicks jumps! He dives to the ground, lies flat on his belly, and starts to roar. No, it's not really a roar—it's more like a little growl. It sounds like squeaking, but the crow has been warned:

This polar bear might bc littlc, but he will defend himself.

Quickly, Vicks searches for a safe spot close to his mother.

Help!
For the first time in his life, Vicks sees a crow. Grrr! He isn't scared. Well, maybe just a little...

The first swim

It's Vicks's first day outside when his mother starts to teach him how to swim. Obediently, he follows her to the water. Then he stops. The water looks dark and deep. *Splash!* Vicks's paws get wet. It feels funny, but good, too. Before long, the cub's back and belly are in the water. And then he gets his head wet! He swims slowly around his mother, paddling his big feet. Congratulations, Vicks! You're a great swimmer!

White or black?

Polar bears have white fur,
but they actually have black skin.
See Vicks's dark nose?
That's the color of his
whole body under all that fur.
If you shaved a polar bear,
it would be entirely black.

"Mama, will you help me out of the water now?"

Shaking like a wet dog

That's the way to dry your fur

Vicks's first swimming lesson is over and he is back on dry land, but his fur is sopping wet. Polar bears know a good trick to get dry—they shake like a dog! Vicks stands firmly on the grass, takes a deep breath, and starts to shake with all his might! Everything is moving: His head, his back, and his bottom. It only takes a couple of moments and then Vicks is completely dry. Well done, Vicks!

Second cousins

Polar bears are part of a large species, or family, of bears. There are black bears, brown bears, koala bears, and panda bears. Vicks won't see his second cousins because they are all living in other parts of the world in warmer climates. They don't like the cold, so they won't be visiting!

Too little to catch a fish

Polar bears eat a lot of fish. They don't buy it in a shop, of course, they go and get fish out of the water with their claws. It's quite a chore. Vicks's mother shows her son how he has to do it. She climbs up on a rock, bends forward, and slaps her paws in the water. When she sits up, she's holding a fish between her paws! But the rock is too high for Vicks to reach the water. When he's bigger, Vicks will become a good fisher, though. For now, he will eat the fish his mother catches for him.

Full tummy
Vicks has to eat a lot
to grow. In one day,
he eats more than ten fish.
Delicious!

Mother allows anything

Oh, what is Vicks doing now? He's chewing and sucking on his mother's head.

He likes her ears. Or her big nose, but he can't quite reach that yet.

And what does his mother do? Do you think she gets mad? Not at all.

She stays quiet and still, and even turns her head so Vicks can reach it easily.

She knows this is how polar bear cubs soothe and comfort themselves.

Lucky Vicks, his mother allows him to do anything he wants!

Male or female?

Because of their thick fur, it is very hard to tell whether a polar bear cub is a male or female. Vicks is a male, because he pees down. Females pee straight behind them.

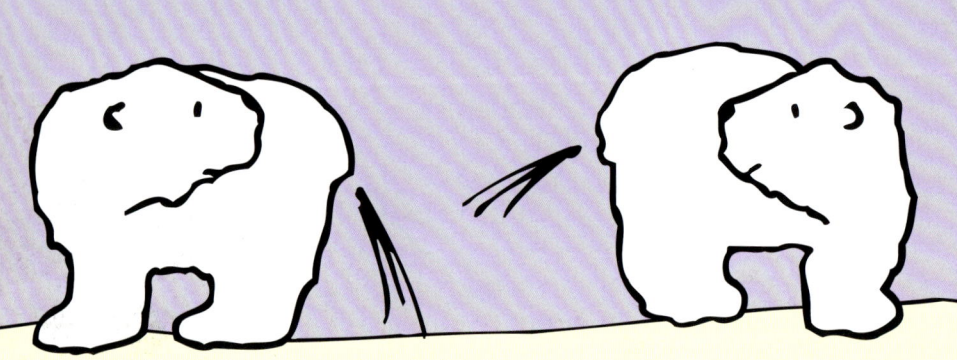

Tough little guy

Bigger and stronger every week

Take a look at Vicks now. He is getting bigger and bigger. His snout is getting bigger, his body longer, and his legs stronger. Vicks is no longer a baby, but a tough little guy. And what do tough polar bears do?

They show off their skills. Vicks is going to prove he can do a lot. He walks over to a rock, lifts his paws, and hoists himself up onto the rock. Well done, Vicks!

Climbing champion

At first, Vicks didn't like big rocks too much. But now he can climb them easily. It's so much fun to be big!

Like a fish!
Diving from the highest rock

Vicks has grown even bigger and now he can swim like a champion. He climbs high rocks and dives into the water. At first, he used to float on the water and he couldn't dive deeply. But now he knows how to dive very well. He uses his big paws like flippers and with a couple of powerful strokes, he reaches the bottom of the deep water. The water is as deep as eight polar bears standing on top of each other, but Vicks doesn't mind. He feels like a fish!

Teasing ducks
At first Vicks was scared of birds, but now that he's bigger, he likes to chase them. He only teases them a little and he doesn't catch them.

"Look, mama, watch me dive to the bottom!"

Happy birthday!

Doing tricks for the visitors

Hurray, Vicks is one year old! From a blind and deaf little white ball, Vicks has turned into a sturdy and strong bear. He can do almost everything: run, play, growl, climb, and dive. And he can do some tricks for visitors! Under the water is a big wall of glass through which visitors can see Vicks swim. When he sees children, he dives, darts, somersaults, and does headstands! Hello, children! Hello, Vicks!

Little cubs

When Vicks is two years old, he will be mature enough to find a mate and have a cub of his own. That little polar bear cub will be born a blind and deaf little white ball who will grow up to explore and enjoy the world. Just like Vicks!

First published in Belgium and Holland by Clavis Uitgeverij, Hasselt – Amsterdam, 2012
Copyright © 2012, Clavis Uitgeverij

English translation from the Dutch by Clavis Publishing Inc. New York
Copyright © 2013 for the English language edition: Clavis Publishing Inc. New York

Visit us on the web at www.clavisbooks.com and www.rotterdamzoo.nl/en/

Vicks, The Polar Bear Cub written and illustrated by Mack
Pictures: Rob Doolaard, JW Borleffs, Sander van der Wel, Cynthia den Uijl, Ronald van Oorschot, and Fedor Nap
In collaboration with the Foundation Royal Zoo of Rotterdam, the Netherlands
Original title: *Vicks. De eerste stap, duik en grom van het liefste ijsbeertje van de hele wereld*
Translated from the Dutch by Clavis Publishing

ISBN 978-1-60537-154-2

This book was printed in March 2013 at Proost, Everdongenlaan 23, 2300 Turnhout, Belgium

First Edition
10 9 8 7 6 5 4 3 2 1